Vol. 2

D1713048

No. 4

Junior Bible Class⁺

FALL QUARTER   **September, October, November 2024**

Editor in Chief:
James M. Leonard, Ph.D.

Managing Editor:
Michelle Birtasevic

Writers:
Union Gospel Press Editorial Staff

ISBN 978-1-64495-601-4

Price: $3.79 per quarter*
*shipping and handling extra

Edited and published quarterly by
LIFESTONE MINISTRIES | UNION GOSPEL PRESS DIVISION
Rev. W. B. Musselman, Founder

Dear Juniors,

Welcome to our new *Junior Bible Class*⁺! We hope it helps you get excited about learning and applying God's Word!

Here are some of the new features:

- The **Big Idea** highlights the main point of the lesson.
- **Discussion Questions** are interjected within the lesson to help you interact with the topic.
- The main ideas are **bold** in the lesson to help you see them at a glance.
- The **Big Question** addresses some doubts, fears, or concerns you may have about God, His Word, or life in general.
- **Next Steps** give you ways to be doing what the lesson is teaching throughout the week.
- **Christ Focus** shows how every lesson points to Jesus.
- **Talk About It** gives you ideas on things to discuss with trusted adult Christians in your life.

DANIEL HONORS GOD'S LAW

Lesson Text: Daniel 1:8-21

"But Daniel purposed in his heart that he would not defile himself with the portion of the king's meat" (Daniel 1:8).

☀️ **BIG IDEA:** Daniel and his three friends honor God with their choice.

DANIEL 1:8 But Daniel purposed in his heart that he would not defile himself with the portion of the king's meat, nor with the wine which he drank: therefore he requested of the prince of the eunuchs that he might not defile himself.

9 Now God had brought Daniel into favour and tender love with the prince of the eunuchs.

10 And the prince of the eunuchs said unto Daniel, I fear my lord the king, who hath appointed your meat and your drink: for why should he see your faces worse liking than the children which are of your sort? then shall ye make me endanger my head to the king.

11 Then said Daniel to Melzar, whom the prince of the eunuchs had set over Daniel, Hananiah, Mishael, and Azariah,

12 Prove thy servants, I beseech thee, ten days; and let them give us pulse to eat, and water to drink.

13 Then let our countenances be looked upon before thee, and the countenance of the children that eat of the portion of the king's meat: and as thou seest, deal with thy servants.

14 So he consented to them in this matter, and proved them ten days.

15 And at the end of ten days their countenances appeared fairer and fatter in flesh than all the children which did eat the portion of the king's meat.

16 Thus Melzar took away the portion of their meat, and the wine that they should drink; and gave them pulse.

17 As for these four children, God gave them knowledge and skill in all learning and wisdom: and Daniel had understanding in all visions and dreams.

18 Now at the end of the days that the king had said he should bring them in, then the prince of the eunuchs brought them in before Nebuchadnezzar.

19 And the king communed with them; and among them all was found none like Daniel, Hananiah, Mishael, and Azariah: therefore stood they before the king.

20 And in all matters of wisdom *and* understanding, that the king enquired of them, he found them ten times better than all the magicians *and* astrologers that *were* in all his realm.

21 And Daniel continued *even* unto the first year of king Cyrus.

BIBLE LESSON

Do you like tests? Today you are going to learn about Daniel and his three friends who took a ten-day test! It was not an English or math test. It was an eating test. They had a choice about what to eat. Do you know what they chose? Vegetables! First, here is a little background. Daniel and his three friends had been living in the kingdom of Judah. The king of Judah, Jehoiakim, was evil. He didn't follow God. God allowed Babylonian King Nebuchadnezzar to conquer Judah. Nebuchadnezzar's army captured King Jehoiakim, along with thousands of others, and hauled them off to Babylon. The teenagers Daniel, Hananiah, Mishael, and Azariah were among the captives. Those four friends loved God and followed

Him. Sadly, Babylon did not follow the one true God. They worshipped many false gods.

King Nebuchadnezzar decided to put some of the captives into a three-year training program. The training involved learning the Babylonian language and literature, which included stories about their gods. He had the four boys' names changed from those that their parents had given them in Judah to Babylonian names. Daniel's name was changed to Belteshazzar, Hananiah to Shadrach, Mishael to Meshach, and Azariah to Abednego.

An important part of their training was eating food that the king also ate. To us, that probably sounds like the best part, but it was not what God wanted Daniel and his friends to eat. It was not the kind of food that would honor God. Daniel and his three friends wanted to please God in everything.

Should we only eat vegetables and water to honor God?

When Daniel told the king's officer that they would rather eat vegetables and drink water than the food and drinks from the king, the officer became worried that the four boys would look weak compared to other captured teens. The king could have the officer killed. So he said no. Daniel didn't give up, though! He found another official and suggested a test for ten days to see who would be in better health, the vegetable eaters or those who ate the king's food.

Where did Daniel and his friends get their courage? Where can we get courage?

Ten days later, the results from the test were in. Daniel, Shadrach, Meshach, and Abednego were healthier than those who ate the king's food! They honored God, and God made them strong and healthy. Daniel and his friends learned to obey God living at home and while living in Babylon. It takes courage to stand for God when people around you aren't (see Proverbs 1:10).

HOW DO I HONOR GOD WHEN PEOPLE AROUND ME AREN'T?

Daniel was just a little older than you! No matter what kind of situation you live in, the school you go to, the neighbors you have, or how others treat you, God can help you be like Daniel. Sometimes you might want to be cool in the eyes of friends who don't respect God. You might want to follow along and say or do things that are bad choices.

God has given you tools to make good choices. The first tool is the Bible. Read it. Spend time thinking about the verses you read. Another tool is memorizing Bible verses. When something tempts you to make a bad choice, say a verse out loud to encourage yourself to honor God instead. Finally, pray to God about anything, big or small.

TO EAT OR NOT TO EAT

The boys were given the best food and drink in the kingdom. Their meals would have been feasts; however, Daniel wanted no part of it. We don't know exactly why he did not want to eat the king's food. God did have rules for what kinds of food Jewish people were allowed to eat (see Leviticus 11).

Daniel wanted to be obedient, and God kept him healthy. God still wants His people to be healthy. Christians are His people. God created both our bodies and souls. We should try to eat as healthy as we can. Get exercise of some kind (walking and hiking, riding a bike, playing sports). God made your body, and He wants you to take care of it. That is another way to honor God.

NEXT STEPS

The first way to honor God is to trust Jesus as Savior. Next, you should obey His Word. Like Daniel, you should make choices that will let God know that He is more important to you than anything else. Learn Bible verses to remind yourself that God will always help you.

✝ CHRIST FOCUS ✝

Jesus honored the Father with everything He did, including dying on the cross for our sins.

TALK ABOUT IT

Ask some trusted Christian friends and family about how they honor God in their lives.

UNIT I:
Faithful Service of Daniel and Friends

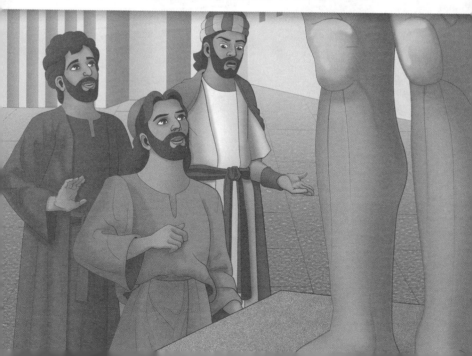

Lesson Text: Daniel 1:8-21

"But Daniel purposed in his heart that he would not defile himself with the portion of the king's meat" (Daniel 1:8).

 BIG IDEA: Daniel and his three friends honor God with their choice.

DANIEL 1:8 But Daniel purposed in his heart that he would not defile himself with the portion of the king's meat, nor with the wine which he drank: therefore he requested of the prince of the eunuchs that he might not defile himself.

9 Now God had brought Daniel into favour and tender love with the prince of the eunuchs.

10 And the prince of the eunuchs said unto Daniel, I fear my lord the king, who hath appointed your meat and your drink: for why should he see your faces worse liking than the children which *are* of your sort? then shall ye make *me* endanger my head to the king.

11 Then said Daniel to Melzar, whom the prince of the eunuchs had set over Daniel, Hananiah, Mishael, and Azariah,

12 Prove thy servants, I beseech thee, ten days; and let them give us pulse to eat, and water to drink.

13 Then let our countenances be looked upon before thee, and the countenance of the children that eat of the portion of the king's meat: and as thou seest, deal with thy servants.

14 So he consented to them in this matter, and proved them ten days.

15 And at the end of ten days their countenances appeared fairer and fatter in flesh than all the children which did eat the portion of the king's meat.

16 Thus Melzar took away the portion of their meat, and the wine that they should drink; and gave them pulse.

17 As for these four children, God gave them knowledge and skill in all learning and wisdom: and Daniel had understanding in all visions and dreams.

18 Now at the end of the days that the king had said he should bring them in, then the prince of the eunuchs brought them in before Nebuchadnezzar.

19 And the king communed with them; and among them all was found none like Daniel, Hananiah, Mishael, and Azariah: therefore stood they before the king.

20 And in all matters of wisdom *and* understanding, that the king enquired of them, he found them ten times better than all the magicians *and* astrologers that *were* in all his realm.

21 And Daniel continued *even* unto the first year of king Cyrus.

BIBLE LESSON

Do you like tests? Today you are going to learn about Daniel and his three friends who took a ten-day test! It was not an English or math test. It was an eating test. They had a choice about what to eat. Do you know what they chose? Vegetables!

First, here is a little background. Daniel and his three friends had been living in the kingdom of Judah. The king of Judah, Jehoiakim, was evil. He didn't follow God. God allowed Babylonian King Nebuchadnezzar to conquer Judah. Nebuchadnezzar's army captured King Jehoiakim, along with thousands of others, and hauled them off to Babylon. The teenagers Daniel, Hananiah, Mishael, and Azariah were among the captives. **Those four friends loved God and followed**

Him. Sadly, Babylon did not follow the one true God. They worshipped many false gods.

King Nebuchadnezzar decided to put some of the captives into a three-year training program. The training involved learning the Babylonian language and literature, which included stories about their gods. He had the four boys' names changed from those that their parents had given them in Judah to Babylonian names. Daniel's name was changed to Belteshazzar, Hananiah to Shadrach, Mishael to Meshach, and Azariah to Abednego.

An important part of their training was eating food that the king also ate. To us, that probably sounds like the best part, but it was not what God wanted Daniel and his friends to eat. It was not the kind of food that would honor God. **Daniel and his three friends wanted to please God in everything.**

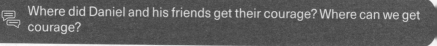

Should we only eat vegetables and water to honor God?

When Daniel told the king's officer that they would rather eat vegetables and drink water than the food and drinks from the king, the officer became worried that the four boys would look weak compared to other captured teens. The king could have the officer killed. So he said no. Daniel didn't give up, though! He found another official and suggested a test for ten days to see who would be in better health, the vegetable eaters or those who ate the king's food.

Where did Daniel and his friends get their courage? Where can we get courage?

Ten days later, the results from the test were in. Daniel, Shadrach, Meshach, and Abednego were healthier than those who ate the king's food! They honored God, and God made them strong and healthy. Daniel and his friends learned to obey God living at home and while living in Babylon. **It takes courage to stand for God when people around you aren't (see Proverbs 1:10).**

HOW DO I HONOR GOD WHEN PEOPLE AROUND ME AREN'T?

Daniel was just a little older than you! No matter what kind of situation you live in, the school you go to, the neighbors you have, or how others treat you, God can help you be like Daniel. Sometimes you might want to be cool in the eyes of friends who don't respect God. You might want to follow along and say or do things that are bad choices.

God has given you tools to make good choices. The first tool is the Bible. Read it. Spend time thinking about the verses you read. Another tool is memorizing Bible verses. When something tempts you to make a bad choice, say a verse out loud to encourage yourself to honor God instead. Finally, pray to God about anything, big or small.

TO EAT OR NOT TO EAT

The boys were given the best food and drink in the kingdom. Their meals would have been feasts; however, Daniel wanted no part of it. We don't know exactly why he did not want to eat the king's food. God did have rules for what kinds of food Jewish people were allowed to eat (see Leviticus 11).

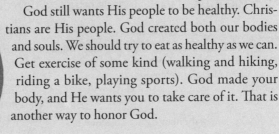

Daniel wanted to be obedient, and God kept him healthy. God still wants His people to be healthy. Christians are His people. God created both our bodies and souls. We should try to eat as healthy as we can. Get exercise of some kind (walking and hiking, riding a bike, playing sports). God made your body, and He wants you to take care of it. That is another way to honor God.

NEXT STEPS

The first way to honor God is to trust Jesus as Savior. Next, you should obey His Word. Like Daniel, you should make choices that will let God know that He is more important to you than anything else. Learn Bible verses to remind yourself that God will always help you.

CHRIST FOCUS

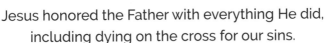

Jesus honored the Father with everything He did, including dying on the cross for our sins.

TALK ABOUT IT

Ask some trusted Christian friends and family about how they honor God in their lives.

Lesson Text: Daniel 3:1, 8-18

"If it be so, our God whom we serve is able to deliver us from the burning fiery furnace" (Daniel 3:17).

 BIG IDEA: Daniel's friends refuse to bow down and worship false gods.

DANIEL 3:1 Nebuchadnezzar the king made an image of gold, whose height *was* threescore cubits, *and* the breadth thereof six cubits: he set it up in the plain of Dura, in the province of Babylon.

8 Wherefore at that time certain Chaldeans came near, and accused the Jews.

9 They spake and said to the king Nebuchadnezzar, O king, live for ever.

10 Thou, O king, hast made a decree, that every man that shall hear the sound of the cornet, flute, harp, sackbut, psaltery, and dulcimer, and all kinds of musick, shall fall down and worship the golden image:

11 And whoso falleth not down and worshippeth, *that* he should be cast into the midst of a burning fiery furnace.

12 There are certain Jews whom thou hast set over the affairs of the province of Babylon, Shadrach, Meshach, and Abed-nego; these men, O king, have not regarded thee: they serve not thy gods, nor worship the golden image which thou hast set up.

13 Then Nebuchadnezzar in *his* rage and fury commanded to bring Shadrach, Meshach, and Abed-nego. Then they brought these men before the king.

14 Nebuchadnezzar spake and said unto them, *Is it* true, O Shadrach, Meshach, and Abed-nego, do not ye serve my gods, nor worship the golden image which I have set up?

15 Now if ye be ready that at what time ye hear the sound of the cornet, flute, harp, sackbut, psaltery, and dulcimer, and all kinds of musick, ye fall down and worship the image which I have made; *well*: but if ye worship not, ye shall be cast the same hour into the midst of a burning fiery furnace; and who *is* that God that shall deliver you out of my hands?

16 Shadrach, Meshach, and Abed-nego, answered and said to the king, O Nebuchadnezzar, we *are* not careful to answer thee in this matter.

17 If it be *so*, our God whom we serve is able to deliver us from the burning fiery furnace, and he will deliver *us* out of thine hand, O king.

18 But if not, be it known unto thee, O king, that we will not serve thy gods, nor worship the golden image which thou hast set up.

BIBLE LESSON

King Nebuchadnezzar built a tall, golden statue sixty cubits high and six cubits wide. A basketball court is roughly as long as that statue was high. A nine-story building both would be about the same height as the statue. Why would someone want to make a statue that tall? We'll find out in our lesson today.

What was the king going to do with that giant golden statue? Shadrach, Meshach, and Abednego found out very quickly. King Nebuchadnezzar made up a rule that might have sounded like an invitation to a fun concert at first, but it was not at all! It was dangerous! He commanded that music be played by horns, flutes, and other instruments. When the music started playing, everyone had to bow down and worship the statue. Anyone who did not bow would be thrown into a huge, hot, fiery furnace. There would be no exceptions. **Shadrach, Meshach, and Abednego loved God and followed Him.** Soon their love for God would be tested. Would they bow down to save their lives?

No, they refused to bow and worship the statue. Some tattletales rushed to King Nebuchadnezzar and reported Shadrach, Meshach, and Abednego. They told the king that those three weren't bowing down to the idol. The king was furious! He demanded they be brought to him immediately.

"Is it true?" King Nebuchadnezzar asked. Maybe he couldn't believe anyone would dare disobey. He gave them another chance, and made it very clear what the rules were. He told the three men that when they heard the music, they had to bow down and worship the golden statue, otherwise, they would be thrown into the huge, hot, fiery furnace. Did the king test them this in front of other people? Would it be harder for the three friends to make the right choice if people were watching, wondering what they would do? Then the king mocked God and asked Shadrach, Meshach, and Abednego whether God would ever be able to rescue them from him.

> Do you think Shadrach, Meshach, and Abednego were afraid?

Shadrach, Meshach, and Abednego trusted God. **Together, they told the king that God was able to rescue them from the flames and deliver them from the king's rule.** Then they added something very important to remember. They said that even if God didn't choose to deliver them from the huge, hot, fiery furnace, they still would not bow down! They might have been afraid, but they knew that it was much more important to honor God than to bow down to the idol.

> Do you think they expected God to deliver them from the furnace?

What do you think happened to Shadrach, Meshach, and Abednego? Their story will be continued in next week's lesson.

DO CHRISTIANS TODAY FACE THE SAME TROUBLE SHADRACH, MESHACH, AND ABEDNEGO DID?

Every day, Christians around the world have to make hard choices to follow God, just as Shadrach, Meshach, and Abednego did long ago. If you're a Christian, maybe some people have made fun of you. Of course, that's not nearly as bad as what those three Jewish men had to face. Still, it isn't easy to deal with. God will be with you during those times. Stay strong for Him.

In many countries, it's illegal to worship God and talk about Jesus. You can easily find articles on the Internet about countries where it's dangerous to be a Christian. Take time to pray with your family for those Christians.

TWO ARE BETTER THAN ONE (AND THREE OR MORE IS EVEN BETTER!)

If you know people long enough, they will probably learn that you are Christian. Not everyone will appreciate that you believe and trust in Jesus. But don't worry! God is with you. Read Isaiah 41:10, Joshua 1:9, Psalm 27:1, and Romans 8:31. God is with you always!

The Bible tells us that "two are better than one" (Ecclesiastes 4:9). One way to help you stand strong for God is to make other Christians your closest and best friends. Shadrach, Meshach, and Abednego had one another as friends. Even though we know that God is all we need, the three friends having one another's backs in hard times probably helped a lot. Find other Christians at school and in your neighborhood to spend time with. Encourage and help one another.

NEXT STEPS

Decide now that whenever you are made fun of because of your faith, you will stand strong for God. The trouble Christians face is nothing compared to the blessings God has promised in the future (see 1 Corinthians 2:9). Trust Him, and remember that He never breaks a promise.

CHRIST FOCUS

 Christ stood strong and trusted God and obeyed Him no matter what.

TALK ABOUT IT

Ask a trusted Christian adult about one thing that helped him or her stand for Jesus when it was hard.

Lesson Text: Daniel 3:19-28

> "Blessed be the God of Shadrach, Meshach, and Abed-nego who hath sent his angel and delivered his servants that trusted in him (Daniel 3:28).

 BIG IDEA: Daniel's friends keep trusting God when they are threatened.

DANIEL 3:19 Then was Nebuchadnezzar full of fury, and the form of his visage was changed against Shadrach, Meshach, and Abed-nego: *therefore* he spake, and commanded that they should heat the furnace one seven times more than it was wont to be heated.

20 And he commanded the most mighty men that *were* in his army to bind Shadrach, Meshach, and Abed-nego, *and* to cast *them* into the burning fiery furnace.

21 Then these men were bound in their coats, their hosen, and their hats, and their *other* garments, and were cast into the midst of the burning fiery furnace.

22 Therefore because the king's commandment was urgent, and the furnace exceeding hot, the flame of the fire slew those men that took up Shadrach, Meshach, and Abed-nego.

23 And these three men, Shadrach, Meshach, and Abed-nego, fell down bound into the midst of the burning fiery furnace.

24 Then Nebuchadnezzar the king was astonied, and rose up in haste, *and* spake, and said unto his counsellors, Did not we cast three men bound into the midst of the fire? They answered and said unto the king, True, O king.

25 He answered and said, Lo, I see four men loose, walking in the midst of the fire, and they have no hurt; and the form of the fourth is like the Son of God.

26 Then Nebuchadnezzar came near to the mouth of the burning fiery furnace, *and* spake, and said, Shadrach, Meshach, and Abed-nego, ye servants of the most high God, come forth, and come *hither*. Then Shadrach, Meshach, and Abed-nego, came forth of the midst of the fire.

27 And the princes, governors, and captains, and the king's counsellors, being gathered together, saw these men, upon whose bodies the fire had no power, nor was an hair of their head singed, neither were their coats changed, nor the smell of fire had passed on them.

28 *Then* Nebuchadnezzar spake, and said, Blessed *be* the God of Shadrach, Meshach, and Abed-nego, who hath sent his angel, and delivered his servants that trusted in him, and have changed the king's word, and yielded their bodies, that they might not serve nor worship any god, except their own God.

BIBLE LESSON

Have you ever felt the heat from a campfire? Campfires cannot compare to the heat coming from the fire that Shadrach, Meshach, and Abednego faced.

Nebuchadnezzar's temper was hot too. He would teach them and all the people watching an important lesson—never disobey this king!

"Make the furnace seven times hotter!" he commanded. It looked like it was over for Shadrach, Meshach, and Abednego.

Nebuchadnezzar had seen God work through the three friends before. He had found them to be ten times smarter than anyone else in the entire kingdom (Daniel 1:19-20). He had chosen them to be leaders in his kingdom.

But none of that mattered to the king at that moment. He was furious!

People watched as strong soldiers tied up Shadrach, Meshach, and Abed-

Why was Nebuchadnezzar so angry with the three friends?

nego and threw them into the furnace. But before they hit the floor, it was the soldiers who had thrown them in that were dead from the heat. It seemed hopeless for the three friends. Who could survive the furnace?

They had decided to obey God no matter how bad it might turn out for them. They had chosen the furnace over bowing down to an idol. **Shadrach, Meshach, and Abednego didn't know whether God would save them, but they chose to trust Him no matter the outcome.**

Suddenly the king jumped to his feet. He could not believe what he was seeing. Four people were walking around in the fire. They looked unharmed and free

Have you trusted God when you weren't sure what would happen?

from the ropes that had tied them. He knew he had put three men in the furnace, not four. He said that the fourth one looked like a son of God.

Nebuchadnezzar came closer to the entrance and shouted to Shadrach, Meshach, and Abednego, calling them servants of the Most High God. "Come out!" he commanded.

The three walked out of the fire. A crowd of people gathered around. They all were curious. The fire had hurt them. Not a single hair on their heads, not their skin, and not even their clothing were burned. They did not even smell like smoke! God had protected and rescued them!

King Nebuchadnezzar admitted that God had rescued them. **The three men trusted in God, not knowing the outcome, and would have given their lives to show they loved God more than anything.** Trusting God is not always easy, but He knows all, is all-powerful, and He gives anyone the courage to follow Him no matter the outcome.

WHAT IF MY FRIENDS WON'T ADMIT THEY'RE CHRISTIANS AT SCHOOL?

We do not know for sure whether Shadrach, Meshach, and Abednego were the only ones in all of Babylon who believed in God. But they were the only ones who would not bow and ended up in the furnace that day. Why do you think some of your friends at school don't want to admit they're Christians? They may be afraid of rejection, not being allowed in the popular crowd, or losing out in some way. But nothing is as important as identifying yourself with Jesus. School is only a few years of your life, but your relationship with God is forever. Pray that the believers in your school and at church or home will stand strong and not be afraid of teasing.

THE HEAT OF PEER PRESSURE

The young men in our text could have given in to the pressure and worshipped the statue. There would have been pressure to bow to the idol.

You probably know what peer pressure feels like. When classmates tell you to do the wrong thing, it might be hard to do what is right. When others say bad things about God and Jesus, it can be hard to speak up. Sometimes things can get ugly when you stand up for God.

It might not be easy to take a stand for God, but it's the right thing to do. God will stand with you when you take a stand for Him. He can give you the courage to speak up and stand out. God stayed with the three men in the furnace. He will be with you at home, online, at school, and anywhere you go.

NEXT STEPS

Memorize today's verse or another verse about trusting God. Whenever you have to choose between God or doing something that would not please Him, remembering Bible verses can help you be courageous and trust God, no matter the outcome.

CHRIST FOCUS

 Jesus trusted and obeyed the Father even when His life was threatened. +

TALK ABOUT IT

Talk to a Christian adult about standing up for God when it is difficult.

UNIT II:
Daniel's Faithful Prophetic Ministry

Lesson Text: Daniel 7:9-14

"I saw in the night visions, and, behold, one like the Son of man came with the clouds of heaven" (Daniel 7:13).

 BIG IDEA: Daniel sees and talks about a person in heaven called the Son of Man.

DANIEL 7:9 I beheld till the thrones were cast down, and the Ancient of days did sit, whose garment *was* white as snow, and the hair of his head like the pure wool: his throne *was like* the fiery flame, *and* his wheels *as* burning fire.

10 A fiery stream issued and came forth from before him: thousand thousands ministered unto him, and ten thousand times ten thousand stood before him: the judgment was set, and the books were opened.

11 I beheld then because of the voice of the great words which the horn spake: I beheld *even* till the beast was slain, and his body destroyed, and given to the burning flame.

12 As concerning the rest of the beasts, they had their dominion taken away: yet their lives were prolonged for a season and time.

13 I saw in the night visions, and, behold, *one* like the Son of man came with the clouds of heaven, and came to the Ancient of days, and they brought him near before him.

14 And there was given him dominion, and glory, and a kingdom, that all people, nations, and languages, should serve him: his dominion *is* an everlasting dominion, which shall not pass away, and his kingdom *that* which shall not be destroyed.

BIBLE LESSON

God sent Daniel a vision. Daniel saw a great sea being tossed by winds. He also saw several strange animals, a throne with Someone called the Ancient of Days sitting on it, and Someone else in the clouds called the Son of Man.

Do you know that God the Father and Jesus have always existed? Before the earth was even created, They were alive. When Jesus came to earth as a baby, that was only the beginning of His earthly life. Knowing this can help you understand what Daniel saw.

Back to Daniel's dream. Daniel was amazed and confused by the dream. He had helped explain the meaning of other people's dreams. Everything in King Nebuchadnezzar's two dreams came true (Daniel 2:45; 4:28). This time, Daniel had the unusual dream. He saw a weird-looking lion, a bear, a leopard, and a creature with ten horns. Next, Daniel was in for a big surprise! He saw Someone amazing sitting on an incredible throne.

The Ancient of Days was sitting on the throne. Daniel described the Ancient of Days as having clothing as white as snow, and the hair on His head was white like wool. His throne had flames and wheels of fire. A stream of fire went out from before His throne. Thousands and thousands of angels stood before Him. The Ancient of Days is God the Father.

Then Daniel saw someone he called the Son of Man. Daniel said the Son of Man arrived on clouds and stood before the Ancient of Days.

🗨 Who do you think is the Son of Man?

The Son of Man is another name for Jesus. Jesus often called Himself the Son of Man while He was on earth (see Matthew 12:32; 16:28; Mark 14:61-62; Luke 12:8; John 1:51).

Jesus is the Son of Man because He is both God and human. Do you wonder how that is possible? We must believe by faith that Jesus is completely God and completely man. Jesus is fully God. He is also fully human. He came from heaven to earth and became a human baby. He grew up. He did great things, and He did not sin. He died for our sins and rose again. Then He went back to heaven. That is incredible!

The Son of Man, Jesus, is in heaven, but He will return someday. In his dream, Daniel saw the Son of Man in the clouds. That was a vision of Jesus returning from heaven someday (see Matthew 26:64; Revelation 1:7). He will return, and Christians will live with Him forever.

🗨 How do you think Daniel felt when He saw that vision?

Daniel saw in his dream that the Son of Man, Jesus, will one day stop all evil and He will reign forever. He will receive all glory and honor. Christians worship and serve Him now and will forever. The kingdom of heaven will never be destroyed. Like the Son of Man, it will be forever.

WHY IS IT IMPORTANT THAT JESUS IS BOTH GOD AND MAN?

From the very beginning of the Bible, we learn that God the Father, Jesus the Son, and the Holy Spirit are one. Genesis 1:26 uses the pronouns "us" and "our," indicating that Jesus was present at the Creation. John 17:5 says that Jesus and the Father were together before the world began. Genesis 1:2 adds that the Spirit was also there. Colossians 1:16 states that Jesus created and holds all things together.

If Jesus were not God, He would have been a sinner. A sinner cannot die for the sins of the world. On the other hand, Jesus also had to be fully human. Only a human could die for other humans.

Still don't understand? Don't feel bad. No one fully understand how Jesus is both God and human, but we know He is.

TO SEEK AND TO SAVE

That title sounds like a motto from the military. Actually, "to seek and to save" is what Jesus, the Son of Man, said His mission was on earth. Read Luke 19:10. Jesus called Himself the Son of Man. He came to seek and to save the lost. He didn't come to find lost things like treasure chests. He came to save people who are lost in sin. The first people God created, Adam and Eve, disobeyed God, and sin came into the world. All people disobey God and are sinners.

But Jesus came to live and die for us. Anyone who believes that He died on the cross, was buried, and rose again can be saved. They will live forever with the Lord one day.

NEXT STEPS

Ask a trusted Christian adult to help you use a concordance or search on your computer for more verses in the New Testament about the Son of Man. Is there a pattern for when and how Jesus usually used that name?

CHRIST FOCUS

 Jesus Christ is the Son of Man, who has always existed and will receive all glory and honor forever.

TALK ABOUT IT

Talk to a trusted Christian adult about what it means that Jesus is the Son of Man.

> ## Lesson Text: Daniel 8:19-26
>
> "The vision of the evening and the morning which was told is true" (Daniel 8:26).

 BIG IDEA: Daniel saw a vision that showed what would happen with future kingdoms.

DANIEL 8:19 And he said, Behold, I will make thee know what shall be in the last end of the indignation: for at the time appointed the end *shall be*.

20 The ram which thou sawest having *two* horns *are* the kings of Media and Persia.

21 And the rough goat *is* the king of Grecia: and the great horn that *is* between his eyes *is* the first king.

22 Now that being broken, whereas four stood up for it, four kingdoms shall stand up out of the nation, but not in his power.

23 And in the latter time of their kingdom, when the transgressors are come to the full, a king of fierce countenance, and un-derstanding dark sentences, shall stand up.

24 And his power shall be mighty, but not by his own power: and he shall destroy won-derfully, and shall prosper, and practise, and shall destroy the mighty and the holy people.

25 And through his policy also he shall cause craft to prosper in his hand; and he shall magnify *himself* in his heart, and by peace shall destroy many: he shall also stand up against the Prince of princes; but he shall be broken without hand.

26 And the vision of the evening and the morning which was told *is* true: wherefore shut thou up the vision; for it *shall be* for many days.

BIBLE LESSON

Today's lesson is about prophecy. Prophecies are statements about events that will happen in the future. God gave prophecies to prophets. Prophets were people who spoke God's messages to His people.

Although some prophecies that we read in the Bible sound scary, God doesn't want us to be afraid. **He lovingly gives us a peek at what's ahead, and we know we can trust Him to help us be prepared for whatever happens.**

Why can we trust God?

Daniel was a prophet. He had been living in Babylon since 605 B.C. He was still living in Babylon when God gave him another vision (around 550 B.C.). Daniel wrote what he saw in his dream *before* the events happened. Daniel had no idea what his dream meant, so God sent the angel Gabriel to explain it.

What Daniel saw in his dream represented real future events. First, he dreamed about two animals. The first animal was a ram with two horns. The two horns represented the powerful kingdom of the Medes and Persians. Babylon was de-feated by the Medes and the Persians around 539 B.C. When Daniel was given the meaning of his dream around 550 B.C, it was eleven or twelve years before it happened!

Next, Daniel dreamed about a goat which had a large horn between its eyes. The goat came from the west. The goat represented the king of Greece, who lived west of the Persian Empire. The goat was strong and trampled the ram. Daniel's dream described the Greek ruler Alexander the Great, who conquered Persia around the year 330 B.C.

Gabriel described how the goat grew more powerful, but then its large horn was broken off and four horns grew in its place. Those four horns represented four kingdoms and their kings that rose to power but never became as strong as the one horn. In 323 B.C., young Alexander the Great died suddenly. Four new kings divided his kingdom and took his place.

Gabriel finished explaining the meaning of the dream. From one of the four horns, an evil power grew. That powerful leader hated God. He lied to and hurt God's people. History speaks of the evil leader Antiochus IV Epiphanes, who destroyed the temple in Jerusalem around 168 B.C. He then tried to eliminate God's people. So did the prophecies in Daniel's dream come true? Yes, part of them—382 years after he wrote them down (550 B.C.).

After Gabriel explained the dream to Daniel, he told him the prophecy would take place in the distant future. Parts of Daniel's dream are still future. We can be confident it will all come true, just as the parts about Persia and Greece came true.

Today our hope is in Jesus. Christians know that He is in control of all things. The final victory over evil will be His.

How should Christians show others the hope that is found in Jesus?

WHY DID GOD GIVE PROPHECIES IN THE BIBLE?

Prophecies often have multiple purposes. God wants His people to know about His perfect plans given to them to enjoy life with Him now and in the future. He had Old Testament prophets give clues about a Savior who would be born in Bethlehem, die a horrible death, and come back to life. All of that was fulfilled in the New Testament. Prophecies also help show that the Bible is true. When a future event was talked about in the Bible and then happened later in history, sometimes thousands of years later, it shows that the Bible is true. Some prophecies also give warnings about things and people that are still in the future! We can be confident that they will all come true, just as the rest of the Bible's prophecies have.

IT'S ALL ABOUT JESUS!

There are many prophecies about Jesus throughout the Bible. Jesus fulfilled more than three hundred prophecies! Jesus' life, death, and resurrection are the most important events in history so far. Many prophecies in the Old Testament point toward Jesus in the New Testament.

One example is found way back in Genesis 12:3. God promised Abraham that the whole world would be blessed through him. Jesus is that blessing. He is a descendant of Abraham. In Isaiah 7, we read about a sign God promised to give the world. That sign would be a virgin having a baby boy called Immanuel. Those words were written hundreds of years before Mary gave birth to Jesus, who is Immanuel. From the beginning to the end, the Bible is all about Jesus.

NEXT STEPS

Get help from Christian adults to look for other prophecies in the Bible. For example, look at Matthew 24:15, where Daniel's dream is mentioned among more warnings about future events. God is kind to give us those alerts to help us prepare for the future.

CHRIST FOCUS

 Jesus Christ promises a wonderful future for all who trust Him as Lord and Savior.

TALK ABOUT IT

Ask a trusted adult Christian why the prophecies in the Bible are important.

Lesson Text: Daniel 9:4-14

"We have sinned, and have committed iniquity, and have done wickedly, and have rebelled" (Daniel 9:5).

 BIG IDEA: Daniel prays for Israel and admits that they have disobeyed God.

DANIEL 9:4 And I prayed unto the LORD my God, and made my confession, and said, O Lord, the great and dreadful God, keeping the covenant and mercy to them that love him, and to them that keep his commandments;

5 We have sinned, and have committed iniquity, and have done wickedly, and have rebelled, even by departing from thy precepts and from thy judgments;

6 Neither have we hearkened unto thy servants the prophets, which spake in thy name to our kings, our princes, and our fathers, and to all the people of the land.

7 O Lord, righteousness *belongeth* unto thee, but unto us confusion of faces, as at this day; to the men of Judah, and to the inhabitants of Jerusalem, and unto all Israel, *that are* near, and *that are* far off, through all the countries whither thou hast driven them, because of their trespass that they have trespassed against thee.

8 O Lord, to us *belongeth* confusion of face, to our kings, to our princes, and to our fathers, because we have sinned against thee.

9 To the Lord our God *belong* mercies and forgivenesses, though we have rebelled against him;

10 Neither have we obeyed the voice of the LORD our God, to walk in his laws, which he set before us by his servants the prophets.

11 Yea, all Israel have transgressed thy law, even by departing, that they might not obey thy voice; therefore the curse is poured upon us, and the oath that *is* written in the law of Moses the servant of God, because we have sinned against him.

12 And he hath confirmed his words, which he spake against us, and against our judges that judged us, by bringing upon us a great evil: for under the whole heaven hath not been done as hath been done upon Jerusalem.

13 As *it is* written in the law of Moses, all this evil is come upon us: yet made we not our prayer before the LORD our God, that we might turn from our iniquities, and understand thy truth.

14 Therefore hath the LORD watched upon the evil, and brought it upon us: for the LORD our God *is* righteous in all his works which he doeth: for we obeyed not his voice.

BIBLE LESSON

While Daniel was still captive in Babylon, he never forgot the lessons he had learned as a child. He chose to obey God, even though that went against Babylonian culture. God blessed Daniel's obedience. He raised Daniel up to be a great leader as an adult. Daniel was an example to his people.

Daniel was a prophet. One of the things he had learned to do as a child was to pray. **Daniel took time to pray even though he had a lot of work to do.**

Why do you think it was important that Daniel took time to pray?

Daniel read the prophet Jeremiah's message. He learned it was time for God to set His people free from captivity. He remembered all the bad things

Israel had done and confessed them to God. He also knew that God was fair when He punished Israel for their sins.

Israel had constantly disobeyed God and followed the sinful ways of the people who lived around them.

> What do you think God thought when Israel copied the people around them instead of obeying Him?

In Daniel's prayer, he made sure to name how Israel had failed. **Daniel covered Israel's sins thoroughly in his prayer. He did not try to cover up anything or make excuses.** Daniel wanted God to forgive Israel and to show them mercy. So he confessed their sins, and he confessed his own sins as well.

All people sin. We should confess our sins just as Daniel did, even when we are embarrassed to tell God about what we have done. We should not leave anything out or try to hide things from God.

> Do you put thought into your prayers, or do you rush through your prayers?

Christians should spend time every day reading God's Word and praying. Short prayers are good, but we should also have unhurried and detailed prayers like Daniel's. We can talk to God just as we would talk to a loving father. There are no special words we must use. Honesty with Him is what is most important. He understands us. When we read the Bible and then spend time talking to God, our love for Him and our understanding of Him grows.

Prayer is powerful because God is powerful. Prayer is not a waste of time. It can change how we think of things. Sometimes we do not see anything change, but we should still keep praying and trusting that God is working. Sometimes we get to see the results of our prayers. It is always exciting to see things change after we have prayed.

WHAT SHOULD I DO WHEN I HAVE SINNED?

God's Word answers that question in 1 John 1:9. We learn that when we confess and tell God about our sins, He always forgives us.

Realizing we have sinned and feeling bad that we have sinned is just the beginning. God expects us to confess what we have done wrong. Confession should never just be empty words. Confession should be heartfelt. Sin is serious. Repentance is serious. God wants us to take sin seriously.

Sometimes God disciplines us when we sin. That isn't fun, but one of the good things about God's discipline is that it encourages us not to repeat the sin that caused it. The good news is that God forgives! When God forgives our sins, He completely forgives them. We do not have to continue to feel bad and confess the same sin over and over.

ME, ME, ME, MEEE!

"Me, Me, Me, Meee!" Some singers warm up by singing those words. Sadly, that is how some people pray to God also. When you pray, do you talk to Him only about yourself? It's good to pray for yourself, but you should pray for other people too!

Daniel prayed for others and asked God to forgive all the people of Israel. He could have just prayed that God would forgive him and forgotten to pray about everyone else. He didn't do that. He showed concern for others. He hoped that God would show mercy to everyone.

Daniel did not say that everyone else was a sinner and he was not. He included himself as a sinner along with all of Israel. Read Daniel's prayer again, and then spend some time confessing sin and praying for others.

NEXT STEPS

At the end of the day, do you ever think about the things you did? That can be a good habit. Think through the day. Ask God to forgive you for anything you did that did not please Him. If we confess our sins, Jesus forgives them completely.

CHRIST FOCUS

Jesus has brought forgiveness of sins and salvation to the world.

TALK ABOUT IT

Ask a trusted Christian adult what kinds of things they pray about most frequently.

Lesson Text: Daniel 10:10-19

> "O man greatly beloved, fear not: peace be unto thee, be strong, yea, be strong" (Daniel 10:19).

BIG IDEA: God sends an angel to encourage Daniel and give him strength.

DANIEL 10:10 And, behold, an hand touched me, which set me upon my knees and *upon* the palms of my hands.

11 And he said unto me, O Daniel, a man greatly beloved, understand the words that I speak unto thee, and stand upright: for unto thee am I now sent. And when he had spoken this word unto me, I stood trembling.

12 Then said he unto me, Fear not, Daniel: for from the first day that thou didst set thine heart to understand, and to chasten thyself before thy God, thy words were heard, and I am come for thy words.

13 But the prince of the kingdom of Persia withstood me one and twenty days: but, lo, Michael, one of the chief princes, came to help me; and I remained there with the kings of Persia.

14 Now I am come to make thee understand what shall befall thy people in the latter days: for yet the vision *is* for *many* days.

15 And when he had spoken such words unto me, I set my face toward the ground, and I became dumb.

16 And, behold, *one* like the similitude of the sons of men touched my lips: then I opened my mouth, and spake, and said unto him that stood before me, O my lord, by the vision my sorrows are turned upon me, and I have retained no strength.

17 For how can the servant of this my lord talk with this my lord? for as for me, straightway there remained no strength in me, neither is there breath left in me.

18 Then there came again and touched me *one* like the appearance of a man, and he strengthened me,

19 And said, O man greatly beloved, fear not: peace *be* unto thee, be strong, yea, *be* strong. And when he had spoken unto me, I was strengthened, and said, Let my lord speak; for thou hast strengthened me.

BIBLE LESSON

Do you know what angels do for God? One thing they do is to act as messengers. God often sent angels to give messages to people in the Bible who were called to do important things. Some examples of people who saw angels are Mary, Joseph, and Zacharias.

God sent angels to Daniel multiple times (Daniel 7–9). Once again, God gave Daniel an unforgettable experience. Someone bright and glorious who looked like a man suddenly appeared and began to speak to him. It seemed like the man was a mighty angel.

Daniel was so scared he fell asleep! The angel woke him up, but he could not look at the angel. The angel touched Daniel and spoke kindly to him. He told Daniel that he was greatly loved. Then the angel told Daniel to stand up.

How would you feel if God sent you an angel who told you that you were greatly loved?

The angel told Daniel that God had heard his prayers. **God knew that Daniel had set his heart to know Him.** The angel said that it was important for Daniel to understand the vision God gave him. He was about to tell Daniel what was going to happen to Israel. Daniel is considered an important prophet. Many times, God revealed events to Daniel and other prophets hundreds of years before they happened.

> What would you do if God told you about something before it happened?

The angel told Daniel that he would have come sooner, but he was stopped by a "prince of the kingdom of Persia." That "prince" was a demon. A good and mighty angel named Michael fought off the demon so that the other angel could get to Daniel.

Again, Daniel became very scared. He fell to the ground, unable to speak. The angel told Daniel not to be afraid and to be strong. Then the angel touched him and God gave Daniel strength. The angel again told him not to be afraid. He encouraged Daniel to be at peace and to be strong.

> Why do you think the angel told Daniel more than once to be strong?

Last week, we studied Daniel's prayer for forgiveness. The glorious angel appeared to Daniel in today's lesson in response to prayer. Daniel is an example for all of us. Prayer is not just something we do before meals or before we go to bed at night. **Prayer is talking to God.** That is a great reason to pray faithfully. We can talk to the Ruler of everything whenever we want!

God gave Daniel strength when the angel touched him. **Today the Holy Spirit works in the lives of Christians and gives strength.** When someone trusts Jesus for salvation, the Holy Spirit comes and lives inside that person. The Holy Spirit will help believers be strong when the going gets rough.

WHAT SHOULD I DO WHEN I FEEL DISCOURAGED?

We all feel discouraged at times. Some people face serious problems every single day. Here are some steps to help you when that happens.

1. Remember that you are not alone. If you are a Christian, the Holy Spirit lives in you. You never face anything by yourself.
2. God's Word encourages us. Read verses or Bible stories about what you are dealing with.
3. Pray for strength. Just as He did for Daniel, God will strengthen you.
4. Keep going. Do not give up. Trust that God is working even if you cannot see what He is doing. When you learn to trust God during the hard times, many times (but not always) you will eventually see what God was working on all along.

ANGELS IN THE BIBLE

Many people get some wrong ideas about angels. You should be careful about what you see in movies, on television, and in video games. It is rare that the people who make those get angels right.

You mostly hear about angels during the Christmas season. The Bible has more to say about those mighty beings. Angels were created by God, and they serve Him as messengers (see Colossians 1:16; Luke 2:8-11). They protect God's children (see Matthew 18:10). They carry out tasks given to them by God. Angels also worship the Lord (see Isaiah 6:1-4). They fight against those who hate God and His people (see Revelation 12:7).

The Bible teaches that angels are *not* to be worshipped (see 22:8-9). Only the Lord is to be worshipped. No one and nothing else should be worshipped (see Luke 4:8).

NEXT STEPS

For one week, before you take a step out of bed each day, pray that God will give you strength and encouragement to live for Him. At the end of the week, look back at what God has done!

CHRIST FOCUS

Jesus is the source of encouragement and strength for all Christians.

TALK ABOUT IT

Ask some Christian adults about what they do to find strength in God when life is difficult.

JESUS USES DANIEL'S WORDS AS A WARNING

Lesson Text: Mark 13:14-27

"And then shall they see the Son of man coming in the clouds with great power and glory" (Mark 13:26).

 BIG IDEA: Jesus warns about future judgment that the prophet Daniel wrote about.

MARK 13:14 But when ye shall see the abomination of desolation, spoken of by Daniel the prophet, standing where it ought not, (let him that readeth understand,) then let them that be in Judaea flee to the mountains:

15 And let him that is on the housetop not go down into the house, neither enter *therein*, to take any thing out of his house:

16 And let him that is in the field not turn back again for to take up his garment.

17 But woe to them that are with child, and to them that give suck in those days!

18 And pray ye that your flight be not in the winter.

19 For *in* those days shall be affliction, such as was not from the beginning of the creation which God created unto this time, neither shall be.

20 And except that the Lord had shortened those days, no flesh should be saved: but for the elect's sake, whom he hath chosen, he hath shortened the days.

21 And then if any man shall say to you, Lo, here *is* Christ; or, lo, *he is* there; believe *him* not:

22 For false Christs and false prophets shall rise, and shall shew signs and wonders, to seduce, if *it were* possible, even the elect.

23 But take ye heed: behold, I have foretold you all things.

24 But in those days, after that tribulation, the sun shall be darkened, and the moon shall not give her light,

25 And the stars of heaven shall fall, and the powers that are in heaven shall be shaken.

26 And then shall they see the Son of man coming in the clouds with great power and glory.

27 And then shall he send his angels, and shall gather together his elect from the four winds, from the uttermost part of the earth to the uttermost part of heaven.

BIBLE LESSON

Has anyone ever said to you, "I have good news, and I have bad news. Which do you want first?"? Today's lesson has bad news and good news. What you think is good news or bad news depends on whether you have trusted in Jesus as Savior.

> Which kind of news do you like to hear first? Why?

Hearing the good news first might make it easier to hear the bad news later. Do you remember what "prophecies" are? God gave Daniel visions that showed him things about the future. Daniel lived more than five hundred years before Jesus came to earth. In Mark 13, our lesson text, you will read about a time when **Jesus used Daniel's words from long ago as a warning.**

In Daniel 7, Daniel saw the Son of Man coming in the clouds. Jesus is the

Son of Man. Daniel's vision was a prophecy of something Jesus will do in the future. His coming down in the clouds refers to His coming again from heaven. He will gather all Christians together and take them to heaven forever. That is the good news—if you know Jesus as Savior, that is. **Jesus will gather only those who trust in Him as Savior to live with Him.**

Bad things will happen before the good things. Jesus called the coming bad times "tribulation." **A lot of troubling things will happen in the future before Jesus comes back.**

 Why do you think Jesus wanted people to know what is going to happen in the future?

Jesus wanted to prepare people for what is coming. Jesus warned of a very difficult time that is coming. It will be one of the worst times in history. Jesus described a time of such terrible troubles that people will want to run away to safety as fast as possible.

Jesus did not say *exactly* what terrible things will happen during the coming terrible times. He did say that there will be people who will lie about being Him. Those fake Christs will be able to do amazing things and will try to convince even Christians that they are the Christ. We should not believe anyone who says that he is Jesus Christ.

Jesus also said that the sun and moon will get dark, and stars will fall from the sky. Nothing like this has ever happened before, and nothing like it will ever happen again.

All those things are bad news. It will be especially bad news for anyone who does not trust in Jesus as Savior. **For Christians, the best is yet to come,** even though terrible times are coming. Jesus warned that things will happen, so we know they will.

What can we do to get ready for the terrible times that Jesus talked about?

CAN I BE SURE THAT EVERYTHING THE BIBLE SAYS WILL REALLY HAPPEN?

Christians believe many things by faith. The Bible is full of prophecies. Get a study for your age. Start in Genesis 1. As you read the Bible, you will see many prophecies. Keep reading and you will also see that many prophecies have come true. Make a note of those. Eventually, you will see that hundreds of biblical prophecies have already taken place. (An online search will give lists of fulfilled prophecies.) Fulfilled prophecies can give you confidence in the prophecies that are still to be fulfilled in the future. Every word that He has spoken is true (see Numbers 23:19).

HERE'S HOW TO BE READY FOR JESUS

God wants to show His love to us. He is perfectly good, and people are not. Everyone does wrong things. Everyone sins. Our sins keep us from living with God because He is perfect. But because God loves us and wants to live with us forever, Jesus came to make a way for our sins to be wiped away.

Jesus chose to come to earth. He died on the cross so that we don't have to die for our sins. Jesus takes our sins away and gives us forgiveness. Everyone who believes in Jesus and has their sins forgiven will live with God forever. If you want to live with God forever, trust in Jesus as your Savior.

NEXT STEPS

Jesus will take only His children to live with Him when He returns. Those who are not Christians will not live with Him forever. Have you trusted in Him to forgive your sins and be your Lord? If you have not, ask Him today to forgive you.

CHRIST FOCUS

Jesus will return for His people just as He said He would.

TALK ABOUT IT

Ask a trusted Christian adult about how to trust in Jesus as Savior so that you will live with Jesus when He returns.

UNIT III:

Jonah: A Resistant Prophet

Lesson Text: Jonah 1:7-17

"Now the Lord had prepared a great fish to swallow up Jonah. And Jonah was in the belly of the fish three days and three nights" (Jonah 1:17).

BIG IDEA: Jonah tries to run away from doing what God told him to do.

JONAH 1:7 And they said every one to his fellow, Come, and let us cast lots, that we may know for whose cause this evil *is* upon us. So they cast lots, and the lot fell upon Jonah.

8 Then said they unto him, Tell us, we pray thee, for whose cause this evil *is* upon us; What *is* thine occupation? and whence comest thou? What *is* thy country? and of what people *art* thou?

9 And he said unto them, I *am* an Hebrew; and I fear the LORD, the God of heaven, which hath made the sea and the dry *land*.

10 Then were the men exceedingly afraid, and said unto him, Why hast thou done this? For the men knew that he fled from the presence of the LORD, because he had told them.

11 Then said they unto him, What shall we do unto thee, that the sea may be calm unto us? for the sea wrought, and was tempestuous.

12 And he said unto them, Take me up,

and cast me forth into the sea; so shall the sea be calm unto you: for I know that for my sake this great tempest *is* upon you.

13 Nevertheless the men rowed hard to bring *it* to the land; but they could not: for the sea wrought, and was tempestuous against them.

14 Wherefore they cried unto the LORD, and said, We beseech thee, O LORD, we beseech thee, let us not perish for this man's life, and lay not upon us innocent blood: for thou, O LORD, hast done as it pleased thee.

15 So they took up Jonah, and cast him forth into the sea: and the sea ceased from her raging.

16 Then the men feared the LORD exceedingly, and offered a sacrifice unto the LORD, and made vows.

17 Now the LORD had prepared a great fish to swallow up Jonah. And Jonah was in the belly of the fish three days and three nights.

BIBLE LESSON

Jonah was a prophet from Israel. He brought messages from God to the people of Israel. Jonah was very proud of being from Israel. One day, God told Jonah to do a job for Him. He told Jonah to go to a city called Nineveh. God wanted Jonah to preach to the people because the people of Nineveh were doing many evil things. God could no longer tolerate evil in the great city of Nineveh.

 What do you think God wanted Jonah to tell the people of Nineveh?

Jonah did not want to do what God asked of him. The people of Nineveh were Israel's enemies. Jonah did not want them to receive mercy. He might have even been afraid for his life. He decided not to obey God.

Instead of going to Nineveh, he went to the city of Joppa by the sea. He paid

to get on a ship that was going in the opposite direction to
a place called Tarshish. He thought he could escape God.
**Jonah did not yet understand that people can
never hide from God, no matter where they go.** God
knows all and sees all.

While the ship was sailing on the sea, God sent a strong wind. The ship
was tossed around so much that everyone thought it would break in two. The
sailors threw things over the side. They hoped they could lighten the load and
sail out of the storm. They began to pray to their gods for the storm to stop.

Jonah was sleeping below deck during the storm. The captain found Jonah
and woke him up. He told Jonah that everyone on the ship was about to die.
He told Jonah to pray to *his* God to save them.

> What happened when the sailors prayed to their gods?

God helped the sailors understand that Jonah was the reason for the storm.
**Jonah told the men that he was running away from the Lord, the God of
heaven.** That made the sailors very afraid. They asked Jonah what they should
do so that the storm would stop. Jonah told them to throw him into the water.
They did not want to do that because they knew Jonah would drown. They
tried as hard as they could to row the ship to shore, but the wind was too
strong. They finally understood that if they did not throw Jonah overboard,
they would all die. As soon as they threw Jonah into the water, the wind
stopped and the sea became calm again.

The others on the ship understood that Jonah had been running from God,
the One with power over even the wind and the sea. Because of what they had
just seen, they feared God, prayed, sacrificed, and made promises to Him. They
did not know it, but **God had prepared a huge fish to swallow up Jonah and
protect him for three days and three nights deep down in the sea.**

CAN I TRUST GOD WHEN HE ASKS ME TO DO SOMETHING?

Sometimes Christians believe that God wants them to do something for
Him. God will never ask you to do something that breaks His rules. If you
think you should do something for God but aren't sure it is Him guiding
you to do it, you can pray, read the Bible, and talk to your pastor and other
Christian adults.

It helps to study people in the Bible who God asked to do something.
Remembering their experiences and how God provided for them will build
your faith. God is the same today as He was during their lifetimes. Memorize a verse that speaks to your situation. For example, Psalm 56:3 is a great
verse to remember when you feel weak or are have trouble trusting God.

A LESSON IN LOVE

God is compassionate and full of grace. He showed His love by sending Jesus to die for us. He wants Christians to show love to others. The Bible teaches that God wants believers to be kind both to friends and to strangers. Jesus even taught that Christians should show love to everyone, *even* their enemies. You might wonder how to love someone who picks on you, but you can show love to anyone. If you see the school bully fall and get hurt, be the one to help. If the person picking on you has no friends, maybe you can be his first friend. Share your lunch if someone does not have food. Ask God to help you show love to an enemy.

NEXT STEPS

The next time an authority figure asks you to do something, think about how you should respond. Should you obey? If so, should you obey immediately, or should you take a while? How much are you like (or different from) Jonah in how you respond to instructions?

CHRIST FOCUS

Jesus willingly obeyed God when He died on the cross for the sins of the world.

TALK ABOUT IT

Ask trusted Christian adults to help you come up with ways to show love to others, even your enemies.

Lesson Text: Jonah 2:1-10

"When my soul fainted within me I remembered the Lord: and my prayer came in unto thee, into thine holy temple" (Jonah 2:7).

 BIG IDEA: Jonah prays for God to save him from drowning in the stormy sea.

JONAH 2:1 Then Jonah prayed unto the LORD his God out of the fish's belly,

2 And said, I cried by reason of mine affliction unto the LORD, and he heard me; out of the belly of hell cried I, *and* thou heardest my voice.

3 For thou hadst cast me into the deep, in the midst of the seas; and the floods compassed me about: all thy billows and thy waves passed over me.

4 Then I said, I am cast out of thy sight; yet I will look again toward thy holy temple.

5 The waters compassed me about, *even* to the soul: the depth closed me round about, the weeds were wrapped about my head.

6 I went down to the bottoms of the mountains; the earth with her bars *was* about me for ever: yet hast thou brought up my life from corruption, O LORD my God.

7 When my soul fainted within me I remembered the LORD: and my prayer came in unto thee, into thine holy temple.

8 They that observe lying vanities forsake their own mercy.

9 But I will sacrifice unto thee with the voice of thanksgiving; I will pay *that* that I have vowed. Salvation *is* of the LORD.

10 And the LORD spake unto the fish, and it vomited out Jonah upon the dry *land.*

BIBLE LESSON

Do you like poems? If you said no, did you consider that most songs are poems put to music? If you enjoy songs, you enjoy poetry. The Bible is full of poetry. Today we are going to examine Jonah's prayer. His prayer is written as poetry to help readers understand his experiences and emotions when he was in the sea.

The previous lesson covered the beginning of Jonah's story. Remember how God told Jonah to go to the city of Nineveh and preach God's message to them? What did Jonah do? Jonah did not obey, and he tried to run away by getting on a ship sailing in the opposite direction of Nineveh. God sent a strong that tossed the boat around on the sea. Jonah told the sailors that his God is the God who created the sea and the dry land. He then told the sailors that the storm would stop if they threw him into the water. The sea became calm when Jonah was thrown overboard. God sent a very large fish that swallowed Jonah to keep him from drowning.

Inside the fish, Jonah was in a very dark place. He was afraid. How would you feel if you got lost in a forest at night or were left by yourself in a large building? Jonah probably felt scared and alone. Then he remembered that God was with him.

In the middle of his troubles, Jonah began to pray. Jonah used interesting words to tell how he felt. He said he cried to the Lord because he was afflicted. That means he felt he was in the middle of a huge problem. He was in big trouble and was suffering terribly.

Jonah described the waves and water rushing over him. He said that seaweed was wrapped around his head. He felt cut off from God. He used those poetic words to describe how it felt to be swallowed by the fish. He probably thought he was about to die.

Jonah said that his soul was fainting. That meant he was becoming weak and discouraged. Then he said that he remembered the Lord. Maybe he had literally forgotten the Lord for a short time, or maybe it was a poetic way of saying that he now turned his attention to the Lord. **He focused on the Lord and asked Him for help.** He knew that people who pray to worthless idols do not get any help or mercy. But Jonah knew that God is real, powerful, and loving. **Jonah knew that he was praying to the living God—so he asked God for help and mercy.** God answered him and rescued him from the dangers of the sea by having the fish spit Jonah out onto the dry land.

 Why is it important to know you are praying to the real, living God?

SHOULD I ASK GOD FOR HELP EVEN WHEN I CAUSE MY OWN PROBLEMS?

Imagine your parents told your sister not to play by the stream. If she fell in and called for help, wouldn't you rush to save her? It wouldn't matter that she did something wrong. You would help her because you love her.

Many times, when people do something wrong, they feel ashamed and guilty. This makes them want to hide the truth. But hiding sin is never right. If people do something wrong to you, do you prefer they apologize or pretend everything is fine?

Read 1 John 1:9. If you have done something wrong, tell God right away and ask for His help. Read Hebrews 4:16. God doesn't love to punish people, but we can always come to God because He is a God of grace and mercy. He loves us and wants to help us in our trouble.

HE FORGIVES!

Jonah probably thought he was doomed. Jonah knew that his only hope was God. Even though Jonah probably hoped to get out of the big fish alive, we do not read in Jonah 2 that he asked about that. Instead, He praised God, saying, "Salvation is of the Lord!" God heard Jonah's humble prayer, and the fish safely spit him out.

We all disobey God. We are all sinners. Just as Jonah did, we can call out to God. When we ask God to forgive our sins, He will. Read 1 John 1:9. This verse assures us that God forgives sins when we confess them to Him. The key is to be sincere and, of course, to ask. If we don't ask for forgiveness, we won't get it. Talk with God about your sins. He forgives!

NEXT STEPS

God wants you to talk to Him any time and all the time. Each morning, talk to God honestly, the way you would talk to your family or friends. Thank Him, praise Him, and ask for His help. This week, write down one of your prayers, just as Jonah did.

CHRIST FOCUS

Jesus is God and hears us when we pray.

TALK ABOUT IT

Ask a trusted Christian adult how he or she talks about
a sin with God.

Lesson Text: Jonah 3:1-10

"God saw their works, that they turned from their evil way; and God repented of the evil, . . . and he did it not" (Jonah 3:10).

BIG IDEA: The people of Nineveh stop their evil ways and ask for God's forgiveness.

JONAH 3:1 And the word of the LORD came unto Jonah the second time, saying,

2 Arise, go unto Nineveh, that great city, and preach unto it the preaching that I bid thee.

3 So Jonah arose, and went unto Nineveh, according to the word of the LORD. Now Nineveh was an exceeding great city of three days' journey.

4 And Jonah began to enter into the city a day's journey, and he cried, and said, Yet forty days, and Nineveh shall be overthrown.

5 So the people of Nineveh believed God, and proclaimed a fast, and put on sackcloth, from the greatest of them even to the least of them.

6 For word came unto the king of Nineveh, and he arose from his throne, and he laid his robe from him, and covered *him* with sackcloth, and sat in ashes.

7 And he caused *it* to be proclaimed and published through Nineveh by the decree of the king and his nobles, saying, Let neither man nor beast, herd nor flock, taste any thing: let them not feed, nor drink water:

8 But let man and beast be covered with sackcloth, and cry mightily unto God: yea, let them turn every one from his evil way, and from the violence that *is* in their hands.

9 Who can tell *if* God will turn and repent, and turn away from his fierce anger, that we perish not?

10 And God saw their works, that they turned from their evil way; and God repented of the evil, that he had said that he would do unto them; and he did *it* not.

BIBLE LESSON

It is often not easy to ask someone for forgiveness. You must be willing to admit that you did something wrong before asking for forgiveness. Admitting that you did something wrong and asking someone else for forgiveness is hard, but it is the first step in choosing to do what is right. Asking forgiveness gets easier with practice!

The first time God told Jonah to go to Nineveh to preach, Jonah ran away. But after God miraculously delivered him and Jonah escaped the troubles at sea, God spoke to him a second time. Once again, He told Jonah to go to Nineveh and preach His message to the people in the city. That time, Jonah obeyed.

When Jonah got to Nineveh, he started to walk through it, shouting God's message. He told the people that in forty days Nineveh was going to be overthrown. That meant Nineveh would be destroyed.

Even though Jonah was warning everyone, he probably believed the people might get angry and hurt him for telling them that. Jonah shared God's message anyway. **He warned the people that their evil actions would bring trouble.**

Jonah was in for a surprise. The people in Nineveh did not get angry when they heard God's warning. They believed the message. When the king of Nineveh heard about God's warning, he got off his throne and took off his beautiful robes. He put on sackcloth. Then the king sat down in ashes. He told everyone in the city to stop eating and drinking, and to put on sackcloth. They even put sackcloth on their animals and would not let them eat or drink anything either! Those actions were a way for the people to show they were being humble. They did not look fancy or proud anymore. They looked helpless, poor, and desperate.

The king and the royal leaders told the people to stop doing wicked things and to cry out to God for forgiveness. They said that if everyone repented and turned away from evil actions, God might show mercy and not punish them by overthrowing the city.

Everyone in Nineveh repented and stopped doing evil things. God did not bring disaster to the city. **The people were saved when they believed God's message, humbled their hearts, stopped doing what was wrong, and asked God to forgive them.**

Jesus also came as God's messenger. He warned people about God's judgment for sin. Believe His message, just as the people of Nineveh believed God when Jonah warned them. When you humble your heart, ask God to forgive you, turn from evil, and He will bring you salvation through Jesus. He will always save anyone who repents of sin.

WHAT DOES IT MEAN TO HUMBLE MY HEART BEFORE GOD?

People sometimes use the word "heart" to talk about the part of us that thinks and feels. When people humble their hearts before God, they believe that God is Creator and that He rules over His creation. Read Colossians 1:16. When your heart is humble before God, you want to honor Him instead of choosing your ways. One way to humble your heart before God is to realize that you have sinned against Him and by asking for His forgiveness. Another way to humble your heart before God is to ask for His wisdom and help in everything you do. Read James 4:6. If we have truly humbled ourselves before God, after we ask for forgiveness, we will try to do what He commands, instead of doing the same things we just asked to be forgiven of.

GOD REPENTED?

What does it mean that God repented? Does that mean God changes His mind? But God is perfect, right? He never changes. At first, it doesn't make sense to read that God repented. But let's look at some other verses that explain what's going on. God has promised that if He declares judgment against a nation, but they repent, He will *always* turn away from that judgment (see Jeremiah 18:7-8). He even promised Israel that if He judged them and they repented afterward, He would forgive and rescue them (Deuteronomy 30:1-10).

When God didn't destroy Nineveh, He didn't change His attitude toward sin. He acted consistently with the way that He always does toward anyone who repents. Because Nineveh repented, God changed the way He would act toward them.

NEXT STEPS

Just as you wouldn't keep trash in your house, you shouldn't keep sin in your life. Each morning, ask God to help you do what is right. When you go to bed, think about what you did that day. Ask God to forgive anything you did wrong.

CHRIST FOCUS

Jesus, God's messenger, calls us to turn away from sin.

TALK ABOUT IT

If you have never repented of your sin, ask a trusted Christian adult to help you learn how.

Lesson Text: Jonah 4:1-11

"The Lord is merciful and gracious, slow to anger, and plenteous in mercy" (Psalm 103:8).

 BIG IDEA: Jonah becomes angry when God forgives people Jonah doesn't like.

JONAH 4:1 But it displeased Jonah exceedingly, and he was very angry.

2 And he prayed unto the LORD, and said, I pray thee, O LORD, *was* not this my saying, when I was yet in my country? Therefore I fled before unto Tarshish: for I knew that thou *art* a gracious God, and merciful, slow to anger, and of great kindness, and repentest thee of the evil.

3 Therefore now, O LORD, take, I beseech thee, my life from me; for *it is* better for me to die than to live.

4 Then said the LORD, Doest thou well to be angry?

5 So Jonah went out of the city, and sat on the east side of the city, and there made him a booth, and sat under it in the shadow, till he might see what would become of the city.

6 And the LORD God prepared a gourd, and made *it* to come up over Jonah, that it might be a shadow over his head, to deliver him from his grief. So Jonah was exceeding glad of the gourd.

7 But God prepared a worm when the morning rose the next day, and it smote the gourd that it withered.

8 And it came to pass, when the sun did arise, that God prepared a vehement east wind; and the sun beat upon the head of Jonah, that he fainted, and wished in himself to die, and said, *It is* better for me to die than to live.

9 And God said to Jonah, Doest thou well to be angry for the gourd? And he said, I do well to be angry, *even* unto death.

10 Then said the LORD, Thou hast had pity on the gourd, for the which thou hast not laboured, neither madest it grow; which came up in a night, and perished in a night:

11 And should not I spare Nineveh, that great city, wherein are more than sixscore thousand persons that cannot discern between their right hand and their left hand; and *also* much cattle?

BIBLE LESSON

Have you ever lost something that you cared about? Losing something that you love can be sad. The people of Nineveh were important to God. Even though they were doing evil things, God wanted to show grace and love to them. They were His creation and made in His image. He wanted them to stop doing what was wrong. He did not want them to be destroyed.

God sent Jonah to Nineveh because He cared about the people who lived there. Jonah delivered God's message that the city would be destroyed. When the people heard God's warning, they asked for forgiveness and stopped doing evil things. God forgave them and did not destroy the city.

Jonah was not happy when God saved the people of Nineveh. Jonah was from Israel. The Ninevites had attacked Israel, killed people, and stolen things. **Jonah thought the people of Nineveh were bad people who deserved to die.**

Jonah knew God was kind and merciful. He knew that God would forgive the people of Nineveh if they asked for forgiveness. Jonah told God that was why he ran away in the first place. He did not want God to save Nineveh. He wanted God to destroy the city.

> Why do people find it hard to forgive people who have done wrong things to them?

Jonah was very angry. He told God exactly how he felt. God asked him if it was good to be so angry. After talking with God, Jonah left the city, set up a little shelter, and sat down. He watched the city, maybe still hoping that it would be destroyed.

It was very hot where Jonah was sitting. God made a plant grow to give Jonah shade. Jonah was thankful to have shade.

The next morning, God had a worm kill the plant, which took away Jonah's shade. The wind blew, and it was a very hot day. Jonah felt weak and angry that the plant had been destroyed. Again, he told God just how he felt. God asked him if it was right to be so angry about the plant. Jonah thought so. He did not think it was fair that God let the plant be destroyed and take away his shade.

Jonah did not work to grow the plant, but he cared about it. God used the plant as a lesson to show Jonah how it feels when something you care about is destroyed. God cared about the people of Nineveh and did not want them to be destroyed either.

> How would you feel if something you made had to be destroyed?

God cares about His creation, even if they have done wrong things. **He wants to save His creation, not destroy it.** That is why He is slow to anger, merciful, and forgiving. That is why He sent Jesus—to bring salvation to His creation and save us from destruction.

IS IT OK TO TELL GOD HOW I FEEL WHEN I'M ANGRY?

Being honest with God about how you feel is important. The Bible records people telling God when they were sad, scared, lonely, or angry. The Lord wants us to pray honestly to Him, even when we are angry or confused (see Psalm 73). Jonah's attitude was not right, but when he got angry, he told God how he was feeling. When he talked to God, God helped him. God showed Jonah that the way he was thinking, feeling, and acting was not right.

God wants to help you too. Read the Bible to learn how God thinks about things. Read Romans 12:2. Ask the Holy Spirit to guide you so that you can follow God's ways instead of letting anger, fear, or selfishness control you.

THEY DESERVE IT! (BE CAREFUL.)

Jonah believed that the city of Nineveh should have been destroyed. He wanted all the people to be judged and punished.

Have you ever watched the news and learned about something bad happening to someone wicked and have been glad about that news? Some people cheer when a wicked person or people get punished. You probably do that sometimes. But while it is true that people who break the law should experience punishment, God wants us to be careful about that attitude.

Find Ezekiel 33:11 in the Bible. God does not feel joy when someone wicked dies. He would rather see wicked people turn to Him and live. Christians should have the same attitude and hope that the wicked of the world would turn to God and live forever.

NEXT STEPS

God wants you to think about things the way He does. You can learn about what God thinks by reading and memorizing what He says and does in the Bible. Read the memory verse every day this week to help you remember what it says about God.

CHRIST FOCUS

 Jesus came to show grace and compassion by dying for us and saving us from destruction.

TALK ABOUT IT

Ask a Christian adult about any time he or she was able to forgive someone who had caused harm.

Lesson Text: Matthew 12:22-32, 38-40

"He that is not with me is against me; and he that gathereth not with me scattereth abroad" (Matthew 12:30).

 BIG IDEA: Jesus says what happened to Jonah gives a hint about how He was going to die and rise again.

MATTHEW 12:22 Then was brought unto him one possessed with a devil, blind, and dumb: and he healed him, insomuch that the blind and dumb both spake and saw.

23 And all the people were amazed, and said, Is not this the son of David?

24 But when the Pharisees heard *it*, they said, This *fellow* doth not cast out devils, but by Beelzebub the prince of the devils.

25 And Jesus knew their thoughts, and said unto them, Every kingdom divided against itself is brought to desolation; and every city or house divided against itself shall not stand:

26 And if Satan cast out Satan, he is divided against himself; how shall then his kingdom stand?

27 And if I by Beelzebub cast out devils, by whom do your children cast *them* out? therefore they shall be your judges.

28 But if I cast out devils by the Spirit of God, then the kingdom of God is come unto you.

29 Or else how can one enter into a strong man's house, and spoil his goods, except he first bind the strong man? and then he will spoil his house.

30 He that is not with me is against me; and he that gathereth not with me scattereth abroad.

31 Wherefore I say unto you, All manner of sin and blasphemy shall be forgiven unto men: but the blasphemy *against* the Holy Ghost shall not be forgiven unto men.

32 And whosoever speaketh a word against the Son of man, it shall be forgiven him: but whosoever speaketh against the Holy Ghost, it shall not be forgiven him, neither in this world, neither in the *world* to come.

38 Then certain of the scribes and of the Pharisees answered, saying, Master, we would see a sign from thee.

39 But he answered and said unto them, An evil and adulterous generation seeketh after a sign; and there shall no sign be given to it, but the sign of the prophet Jonas:

40 For as Jonas was three days and three nights in the whale's belly; so shall the Son of man be three days and three nights in the heart of the earth.

BIBLE LESSON

Jesus sometimes said things that seemed like riddles. One time, He spoke about the prophet Jonah. **What happened to Jonah way back in the past gave a clue about something that would happen to Jesus.**

 What do you remember about the prophet Jonah?

Prophets were individuals who spoke with God, and God gave them messages to give to people. Many of the prophets wrote about a Messiah whom God promised to send one day. That Messiah *has* come—He is Jesus.

When Jesus was on earth, the Jewish people would have known a lot about the writings of the prophets. The important religious leaders, the Pharisees, should have known that the many clues from the Old Testament made it clear that Jesus is the Messiah. Sadly, they did not believe it.

One day, a man who could not see or talk was brought to Jesus. A demon was oppressing him. Jesus sent away the demon and healed the man. He could see and talk again.

When the people saw the miracle, they were amazed. They started wondering whether Jesus was the promised Messiah.

When the Pharisees heard the people talking, they said Jesus was using the power of the devil to heal the man! Jesus explained that if He used the devil's power to set a man free, then the devil would be fighting himself. But if Jesus set the man free by the power of the Holy Spirit, then it was proof that the kingdom of God had come.

The leaders rejected the work of the Holy Spirit. Jesus said it was unforgivable to look at the miracles done by the Holy Spirit and say that they were done by the power of the devil.

Some time later, the Pharisees asked Jesus to show them a sign to prove that God had sent Him. Jesus knew that their hearts were still full of evil and unbelief. He said the only sign they would see was the sign of Jonah the prophet. He said that Jonah was in the belly of the fish for three days and three nights and that the Son of Man would be buried in the earth for three days and three nights. **Jesus was giving the people a clue that soon He would die, be buried for three days and nights, and then rise again.** God was going to show them the greatest miracle of all—**Jesus rising from the dead.**

🗨 How were Jesus and the prophet Jonah similar?

Jesus told the Pharisees God's message. He did miracles right in front of them, but they did not humble their hearts and ask God to forgive them. Jesus warned them to believe God's message and turn from sin.

HOW CAN I UNDERSTAND THE PROPHECIES IN THE BIBLE?

Bible scholars have counted the number of prophecies in the Bible. Not everyone agrees exactly how many there are. Some estimate that there are about two thousand prophecies in the Bible.

Some prophecies are easy to understand. Read Mark 10:32-34 and Micah 5:2. Other prophecies seem like riddles. You have to think deeply or get someone to help you understand them. When you study the Bible, ask God to show you what it means. Try to read the whole Bible. Ask for a study Bible as a gift. Keep notes. As you read, you will find that many prophecies have already come to pass. When you encounter something you don't understand, get help from adult Christians, such as your parents, teachers, or pastor.

WHO? WHAT? WHY? HUH?

Who are the son of David and Beelzebub?

Son of David is a name used for the promised Messiah. Long ago, God said the Messiah would come. That King would be from the family of King David. Jesus is the One God promised to send. The "son" part might be confusing, because David lived about a thousand years before Jesus came to earth! Often in the Bible, the word "son" was used to describe any male descendant, no matter how many years apart the father and his great-great-great (etc.) grandson were.

Beelzebub was the name of one of the fake gods worshipped by people in nations around Israel (see 2 Kings 1:3). Its name means "lord of filth." Yuck! Beelzebub was so awful that the Jews also called Satan by that name. In Matthew 12:24, the Pharisees were talking about Satan.

NEXT STEPS

Plan on reading through the whole Bible. Are there parts of it you haven't read yet? Get a notebook to write things you don't understand and need to ask someone about. Ask God to guide you and give you an understanding of His Word.

CHRIST FOCUS

Jesus is the fulfillment of the greatest prophecies found in the Bible.

TALK ABOUT IT

If you do not understand how Jesus and Jonah are similar, ask a Christian adult to explain it some more.

REVIEW OF WHO'S WHO

ACROSS

4 person from Media-Persia who conquered Babylon

5 Daniel's friend whose name contains the word for a place you sleep at night

6 a prophet who tried to hide from God

Down

1 Daniel's friend whose name sounds like "my shack"

2 Daniel's friend whose Hebrew name begins with *S*

3 the city where the people were wicked but they repented

4 the prophet who understood a king's dream

Forbidden Food

In the Old Testament, we read about the kinds of animals God did not want the people of Israel to eat. He gave the Jewish people laws to help them know how to please Him. All the laws God gave them, including the rules about what food was not good to eat, were given to keep them pure and different from the people of the nations around them. We are not sure why Daniel did not want to eat the king's food, but we *do* know that Daniel wanted to do things that honored God.

Have some fun learning about some animals God told the people of Israel not to eat. Unscramble the words below. Some pictures are on the page to give you hints.

COCOSLIDER_____   SLOW_____

SGIP_____   LEGSEA_____

BTSA_____   STAR_____

NAVERS_____   LEMACS_____

TRUELUVS_____   ARZLIDS_____

KWASH_____   CALFONS_____

BIBARTS_____

SKORTS_____

Jonah Maze

Help Jonah find his way to Nineveh so that he can preach God's words to the people.

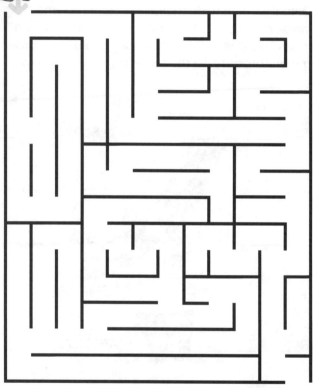